# THE GREATEST OF THESE IS LOVE

**The Greatest of These is Love.**

A collection of poems and prose by David E Murdoch.

Email: davidmpoet@gmail.com

# FOREWORD

Thank-you for purchasing this book.

This is the sixth book I have published and as with each of the previous five books, all proceeds from the sale of this book will be going to a charity.

With this book I am supporting **Action Mental Health** for the excellent work they do in promoting mental wellbeing across Northern Ireland.

I personally know several people who have successfully moved forward on their mental health recovery journey because of the amazing help they received through this excellent organisation.

You can find out more about the work of Action Mental Health on their website at www.amh.org.uk

# About This Book

Since I published my last book in 2022, I had wanted to put together a collection of poems and reflections on the superlative quality of Love.

Beginning with the obvious aspect of mutual love in a marriage, my thoughts turned to other types of love such as love of neighbour, love for the people in our community, self-love, lost love, unrequited love, what we love to do, and the love of God.

Among these poems and personal reflections you, the reader, will find words of comfort, gratitude, humour, courage, and most of all, expressions of love.

I have also included some photographs from our family album, these along with information about my life and my family will, I hope, let you get to know me a little better, both as a person and as a poet.

I always enjoy hearing from the people who read my poetry books, although I apologise in advance that I am not always able to reply to each of you. My email address is davidmpoet@gmail.com

Thank-you,


David E Murdoch
Autumn 2024.

## What is Love in a Marriage?

LOVE is not always about caring, pampering, romantic walks, talks, long drives, cosy dinner dates, holding hands, cuddles, hugs, intimate moments, and sexual union. Yes, for sure, these are some of the things that create special moments and must not be neglected.

But LOVE is also about growth, showing maturity, sorting out problems between each other every time and not giving up. Accepting each person's flaws and helping to overcome them, supporting each other's dreams, valuing their unique qualities. Giving each other adequate space when needed, letting each one voice opinions and listening to their ideas with an open mind. Caring for one another in sickness, trusting them, respecting them for who they are and what they do, showing appreciation for them.

Always be proud of your partner, considering them the best person of your life, your champion and the truest of all your friends.

**For Pauline, My Wife, My Love.**

Every day is beautiful
Not for the sun above
It's because I have you in my life
That each day is filled with love.

Every night is beautiful
Not for the starry sky
But because you are in my life
Makes it beautiful, that's why.

Every sunset is beautiful
When the heavens turn to gold
And because you are in my life
I've someone to love and hold.

Every garden is beautiful
Because of each flower and tree
And having you in my life
That means the world to me!

Every moment is magical
When filled with love and light
And having you as my darling wife
Is the most beautiful delight.

**Thoughts Penned After Attending a Family Wedding.**

It doesn't seem that long ago you were a little child
Now we see a stunning beauty walking up the aisle
The choice you've made to choose this man
And accept the ring he places gently on your hand

We remember your youthful squeals of laughter
As you seriously agree to this happy ever after
We think of your intensity all those years at school
Your groom looks quite nervous yet you're looking cool

And after the photos, the speeches, and the cake
As everyone hugs and each hand gets a shake
For better or worse, whatever the weather
You and your companion will face it together.

For children grow up so fast it appears
Suddenly a teenager so quickly the years
Then in a blink they've flown from the nest
It's at the wedding we know they're blessed

The woman a wife, her husband beside her
An occasion that other dear friends get to share
Pray happiness, health, plus joy, with long years to follow
On this special day and on into tomorrow.

**A Lifetime of Love is Something Very Special.**

Love is like a giftbox wrapped in ribbon
Something a lover is often given
Held together with glue not nails
Full of successes, full of fails.
A lifetime of hurt and pain and smiles
In a mosaic of different stylish tiles
Little events each inter-locking
The happy, sad, the downright shocking.

The hospital waits, the holiday times
The cuts and scratches, the nursery rhymes
Food, dishes, shopping, growing bills
School runs, mowing grass, kiddies' ills,
Broken hearts, ecstatic intimate bliss
Mixed all together with bits of this
Exam stress, job searches, rent or rates
Do it yourself, and perpetually wonky gates.

The ordinary everyday, happy, sad,
It makes you thankful and extremely glad
That you have been given something priceless
And looking back can see the rightness.
Of this box of love, indeed a treasure
A container of everything for your pleasure.
Cheer if you've been treated well,
For other people go through hell.

Their relationships, they crash and burn.
Every time they take a turn
Dysfunctional families, broken home
They could likely write a tome!
So, you, if happiness overall has been your life
Embrace your husband, kiss your wife.
Cherish what you have in your memory box
Do not count the time with ticking clocks.

No. It is an incredibly special gift,
The like of which gives you a lift
So, never treat it like common chaff
Never excuse it away with just a laugh.
Honour your box of love enduring

Continue to give in this way securing
A treasured soul-shared special life
Full of good things, rarely strife.

At least as you look back down the years
You'll not be shedding many tears
You'll have made your milestones side by side
Hand in hand throughout the ride,
When as eyes dim and a lifetime ends
May you be surrounded by many friends
Those with whom you made a genuine connection
Who will always remember you with deep affection.

**Love Is the Greatest Gift.**

Hands are held together
Hearts entwined with love
Familiar thoughts of family
Are blessings from above,
The happy gift of friendship
As well as those memories dear
Carry us through the bad days
At this gloomier time of year.

Our lost loved ones' anniversaries
Coincide with skies both dark and bleak
When hearts weigh heavy in sadness
And we'd much rather cry than speak,
This is the time for friendship
Moments to be held and hugged
Acknowledge others do care for us
Reminders of such precious love.

As dormant bulbs are buried
In autumn's warmer loam
The new growth appears in springtime
And brightens up our home,
This too for blossoming friendships
With companions from long ago
Who willingly will give encouragement
Because they love us so.

"God is Love" the scripture tells us
And cast in God's image are we
Daily we can reflect His precious love
To share with friends and family
Be here for one another
For us, and also for you
With empathy, comfort and kindness
Together we'll find a way through.

**Remember.**

There are 3 gifts
That are always welcome
No matter when you give them
Be it on a special occasion
Or as a present for
Any day at all.


They are the gift of self,
The gift of time,
And the precious gift of Love.

**A Poem for Our Anniversary Week in March.**

The fact of the matter is simple
Whatever goes on with the weather
Us two teddy bears are deeply in love
And like to keep spending time together.

The weatherman's saying it might snow soon
They're calling it the "Beast from the East"
Hey, we'll snuggle up in our duvet and go spoon
When you're in love weather matters the least.

**A Journey to Recovery.**

If you trust me, hold my hand
Let me take you somewhere new
Leave behind the swirling thoughts
At least for now, an hour or two.

Do not let go of my outstretched fingers
This is a journey of turns and twists
I promise you we'll take it together
Don't give up, these things resist.

Guilt, anger, sadness, hurt,
Low self-esteem, self-hate and worse.
Broken relationships, death, shattered promises.
All emotions which make you cry and curse.

See them passing, note their colour
Black, green, red, disgusting brown
Like going through a ghost train ride
Scream at them or knock them down.

Now into the open fresh and clean
Breathe in deeply, smell the air
See how blue the sky above us
Look about you everywhere.

Let us walk in the glorious sunshine
Let us bathe in the clear fresh stream
Let us taste the sweetest berries
And serve them up with bowls of cream.

My friend you ask, "Where are we presently?
For the contrast is so great
If I could I'd stay here forever
Start my life with a brand-new slate…."

"Where is this?" I hear you ask me
"I'll tell you my friend, you know I would.
This is the place we call Recovery
Where wellness happens and life feels good."

When we return to your daily routines
And you know of course that soon we must
Stop, stand straight, and make a decision
Remember it begins with a matter of trust.

One step at a time is all that's needed
Keep before you the vision of New
Ask for help, seek out the answers,
In time you'll see a recovered you.

The past becomes like a distant country
Remembered in flashes, if at all
You are on the road to Recovery
Even if you might sometimes fall.

A new chapter is being written
Putting those toxic days behind
And realise I'll never leave you
Reach out and my hand you'll always find.

One day, I promise, you will discover
That you no longer want to harm yourself
You have located the place to recover
From this point on in better health.

Relax, enjoy, yes smell the roses.
Dig down deep and refresh your soul
And after time, you can outstretch your fingers
To help someone else achieve this goal.

## A Widow's Lament.

Who will share this day with me
To watch the sun settle down in the western sky
Slip below the horizon into the sea?

Who will tightly hold my hand
As I walk into a warm room of open fires and crimson wine
To mull over the day's events?

Who will join me in the warmth of love
Beneath a fleecy duvet in a king-size bed and caress me tenderly
Until deep sleep comes?

Sadness permeates my very soul since I lost you
Taken from this life so prematurely, how I wanted to share this day and
thousands more with you
But you have departed leaving me all alone.

**Let's Be Here For One Another.**

The sky isn't always blue
Clouds often block the sun
Our mood may change from day to day
When our head tells us to run.

Bills need paid yet money is scarce
Food prices are definitely soaring
Our shoes are worn, our clothing patched
The roof leaks when rain is pouring.

And yet again our heart is true
We have health, at least a measure,
Surrounded by those we truly love
Dear friends and family we treasure.

If age and health or life in general
Is dragging you down low today
Remember please we care for you
And we're only one phone call away.

After each storm, the sun comes out
Together, we can face your fear
Love, they say, makes the world go round
We're here for you, we're here.

**The love of my life is Pauline, my wife.**

## Togetherness.

The grass is green
The sky is blue
The two of us
That's me and you.
The time is now
This moment bright
The two of us
Will be alright.
The sun's above
The earth's below
The two of us
Will take it slow.
In things mundane
Or times with prayer
The two of us
Will also share.
In storm, in calm
There's still a plus
That's you and me
The two of us.

## I'm Moving Gently Downstream.

I was struggling with thoughts of my past experiences
That weighed me down as much as marble slabs
Memories of friends who had deserted me
In full-blown distress when I needed them all

I sat dejectedly on the bank of a sluggish river
Watching the oiliness of the water's surface
It looked as if it wasn't even flowing, except
I could see from the floating leaves it was

"Tell me" I asked of this slowly moving fluid
"Do you look forward to the place you are going
Or back to underground springs that gave you birth?"
The river glinted in a sudden ray of sunshine

As if it was winking and smiling at my query
I felt as if an answer was borne in the air
Perhaps by the ancient invisible spirit of place
"I am what I am in this moment that I am."

It was a flash of enlightenment and truth
The river was being honest and clear for me
It was neither the ocean, lake, nor spring
It could only be what it was now. A river.

And appearing in that moment of clarity
I saw my life for what it was at this time
Flowing steadily, taking me gently forward
"I am where I am, in this moment of time."

**To The Daughter Who Never Lived.**

I am thinking of the first time I held you
My hands looked big and awkward beside your tiny frame
"Hello you" I remember saying
To which you scowled sleepily
Briefly opening then closing your eyes
I was nervous about it, you were so fragile, so very small
Then your tiny perfectly formed little left hand reached out
And clutched my index finger tightly
As if to say, "it's alright Daddy, I won't ever let you go."
My heart was overflowing with love
As I gently kissed the top of your little head
"I'll never ever let you go either my sweet" I told you,
With all the certainty of innocence…

At least, that is how I see it happening in my dreams
We never got that far, did we?
You didn't arrive to the bright light of life
I never got to cradle you in my big clumsy hands
Or kiss your tender little head
We don't have pictures of you dressed up in clothes
Knitted by an adoring aunt
For all the wishes that we did,
We don't have you.

'Blessed are those who mourn
For they shall be comforted'
Except we never will be comforted
Wishing you were here, and knowing that you're not
Only ever meeting you in our saddest nighttime dreams
Where you live and breathe
Only to leave again
When the morning alarm clock
Wakes us from our slumber.

**What is an Amateur?**

Words fascinate me, they always have done.

For this gift I thank my parents especially my mother who, as a teacher, was interested not only in the meaning of a word but in its origin or the etymology of the word. She had a much-thumbed green etymological dictionary and would often stop while reading an article to see what she could learn about a particular word she hadn't come across before. And later, if time permitted, she'd go on to explore the background history of that word.

Perhaps this is why I enjoy it so much playing word games such as Scrabble© and why I ended up spending a large proportion of my working life as a proofreader, a researcher, and an instructor.

From quite an early age even before I went to school, I had been taught by my parents to read. Reading still gives me pleasure to this day, and I confess that yes, I am a bit of a book hoarder.

My father, as an ordained minister and subsequently as a missionary in Brazil, was diligent in picking the correct word when he was speaking to a congregation or delivering talks at large public gatherings. My sister Sharon was born in Brazil, but I was born after my parents had to return to the United Kingdom because of serious illness.

When I was quite young, I can remember poring over my father's copy of his Greek Interlinear of the Christian Greek Scriptures along with Vine's Expository Dictionary of New Testament Words fascinated by the depth of meaning in a single simple English word.

To this day, if I am invited to visit someone in their own home, I'll often end up perusing the books on their bookshelves, wanting to see if perhaps we have common interests in the subjects to be found there.

Now, let me bring us back to the topic in hand, and ask the question; What is an AMATEUR?

Obviously, many people would immediately say that an amateur is the opposite of a professional. However, that places the emphasis on the word "professional".

Instead, let us focus our attention instead on this word "amateur" which is a French word. It has the literal meaning of "for the love of" or "one who loves".

Perhaps you can paint pictures, and while it gives you a great deal of pleasure you would never dream of putting your paintings on show or in an art gallery. If I suggested it, you would probably exclaim, "that's only for professional artists!" You likely put yourself down when describing yourself by saying something along the lines of "Who me? No, I'm only an amateur."

The same might be true of writing a poem, or putting together a flower arrangement, or baking a cake, crocheting or knitting a garment, or indeed anything else you enjoy doing.

But let me be straight with you now. You should NEVER ever put yourself down.

Why? Because you are doing something that you love!

Yes, you are an amateur - a genuine lover - and that is nothing for you to be ashamed of when telling other people.

You are a creator, a composer, a maker, a poet, a knitter, a writer, a painter, a baker, and so on, for the simple reason that what you have taken up is for your enjoyment. You are doing it for the LOVE of doing it. You are an amateur in the true sense of this word.

You are an amateur! Isn't that wonderful and worth celebrating? You are one who loves, and who "for the love of" brings something new into existence. Surely that experience brings you immense joy!?

I know it does me, because I also am "one who loves". I am a poet, a weaver of words.

Yes, I too am an amateur.

**A Final Goodbye to a Dear Friend.**

The birds are singing in their morning
As dawn's first light is breaking
And today we lay you down to rest
Into the earth's sweet caress.

Let's hope there's singing in our mourning
For our hearts they are breaking
When will we again have rest?
Once your sweet head we cannot caress.

This day will be forever fixed
In our minds and for our friends
We will not have you in our midst
Yet you will be here until the very end.

This is a tragedy that cannot be fixed
Our fondest memories we have deeply mined
Your presence will linger like the morning mist
We will not forget you ever my dear friend.

**For You, My Friends, With Love.**

I'm writing a poem for all my friends,
I know how it begins but not how it ends.
You pick me up when I'm feeling blue,
And hopefully I do the same for you.
You tell me your troubles, yet listen to mine
We share each other's stories when everything's fine
Together we're stronger, of that I've no doubt
You know if you need me to just give me a shout
If I'm down I may not reply, if I'm well I sure will
I love hearing your news it gives me a thrill
Funny pictures, cartoons, and those terrible jokes
Won't detract me from liking you special folks
Therefore, let us continue to build and support
Because we have this unique friendship rapport
I'll help you as you are helping me
And if there's ever a chance, let's meet up for tea.

Best Wishes one and all.

**A Poem Written to Every Man.**

Did you know there are two verses written especially for husbands that are found in the Bible in the Letter to the Ephesians?

EPHESIANS 5:28

"In the same way husbands should love their wives as their own bodies. A man who loves his wife loves himself, for no man ever hated his own body, but he feeds and cherishes it."

and

EPHESIANS 5:33

"Nevertheless, each one of you must love his wife as he does himself; on the other hand, the wife should have deep respect for her husband."

I was thinking about these two verses and decided to compose a piece of poetry. I hope you will like it and appreciate the message.

**One Man's Reflection on Women based upon Ephesians Chapter 5.**

When God created woman
He made a perfect one,
He picked the finest qualities
And wove in lots of fun.
He clothed her skin with beauty
Filled her heart with emotions too,
He poured in heaps of sweetness
Her inner strength renewed.
He made her to be mother
To nurture all her young
And looked at her with pleasure
The human race begun.

So, when you look at women
Be it mum, or child, or wife,
Remember she's made to God's design
Go cherish her in your life.
She was to be the other half
To make a man's life whole
So, men, if married, treat her well
Her virtues please extol.
Tell others of her qualities
But most of all tell her,
And faults you should just forget
For of your own you're well aware.

If married, say "I love you"
Then show her from your heart
For that's why you joined together
And hope you'll never part.
God's plan is always perfect
It's we who make mistakes
But recalling who designed the woman
Is usually all it takes.

"Being a man" is not being macho
"Being a man" isn't a bully thug
"Being a man" doesn't take millions,
"Being a man" is simply showing love.

**Who Do You Have Beside You?**

This world is full of people, some who'll do you harm
Others with a sweet sickly smile will turn on lots of charm
But when you start to crumble, and everything seems so black
The friends you need around you are those who have your back.

The people who make time for you and listen to your woes
Without making any judgements or treading on your toes
They give support and succour and pick you up again
They're the ones who help you to rise above your pain.

Most likely you've been there for them, and they know it too,
Unlike the talkers and the moaners, they'll come through for you.
When life seems like a burden, and you struggle up the road
True friends come in beside you and help you with your load.

Treasure such special people for they're as rare as gold
By keeping them in your circle you'll get returns tenfold.
Ignore the biters and the fighters, and the ones who couldn't care
Let those know that you no longer want to see them there.

Fill your life with people whose memories you'll always treasure
Who, even when things are bleak, the sight of them gives pleasure.
Life is short, the road is hard, and one day it all ends
Until that final curtain falls, hold on to such dear friends.

**How Much Do I Love You?**

"How much do you love me?", she asked one day.
And I replied, "In every way.
I love your hair and the way you smile
I love you darling mile after mile
I love your scent after a bath
I love the way you make me laugh
I love your touch and your kisses too
I love you forever baby, I really do!
I loved you then and I love you still
For the next million years you know I will...."

"I'm glad sweetheart," says she to me,
"So will you get up and make some tea?"

## Admiring the Beauty of a Fallen Leaf Lying on the Ground.

Far from its mother
A fallen leaf
Poses beautifully
Against a grey curtain.
Even in decay
She is an artist's palette
Of nature's colour.
Fallen Gold
A rich treasure chest
Of autumn hue
Ignored by many.
Stop, don't walk by
Open your eyes and you'll see
The wonders of a once-a-year
Miracle unfolding itself.
For all around you
Is an awakening of spirit
And a glimpse of the Divine
In the beauty of a fallen leaf.

## David: It's just me!

It's just me. I know.
I genuinely like wishing everyone I meet that they will have a pleasant day.
I honestly like being kind.
I like holding the door open for the person coming up behind me. I like offering to help carry something for them if my hand is free.
I like smiling at strangers in public. I like saying "hello" to the person who is behind or in front of me in any queue.
I like chatting to the person on the checkout, and if they have a badge to call them by their name when I say "thank-you".
I like helping the person with the pram if there is a step up or a high kerbstone and they are clearly struggling.
I like giving out compliments. I like showing people how much I value their assistance.
I like making someone feel appreciated and seeing their smile. It gives me a warm happy feeling inside.
And even if I get a grumpy grunt in response, I still smile. After all, I don't know what this person is struggling with currently in their life.

Good manners cost us nothing, but in this me-first, selfish world where they seem to be a rarity, showing them to other people can really make someone else's day!

It pays to be this way because, although you don't expect anything back in return, often you will receive it.

Jesus is recorded in the Bible as saying, "love your neighbour". And in what has become known as the 'Golden Rule' we're all encouraged by Jesus simply to treat one another as we would like to be treated ourselves.

It really is that simple. I know that I like to be treated with kindness and love. To be pleasant to people needs no other reason than because that's what I want to be.


The Golden Rule - Matt 7:12, Luke 6:31.  Love of Neighbour - Mark 12:31.

**You Are Loved.**

In the colder days and nights of winter, it is easy to find yourself thinking about the things you don't yet have - but instead, I ask you to reflect on what you have in abundance in your life.

A measure of health, a roof above you, a blanket for warmth, food to eat, and most of all a circle of friends who love you for who you are not for what you possess.

You are a star for many. A bright beacon of light in a very dark world. A person they can confide in and know that you will listen without judgement. A friend who won't gossip behind their backs about them to others.

You are all of that and more to each one of them, as they are to you as well.
You have been surrounded by blessings. You have the gift of friendship.

Yes, some things are lacking in your life. Yes, some dear loved ones no longer walk beside you. Yes, your mind, at times is troubled with sadness. There is no shame in admitting that fact, I know I do.

But count your blessings. Look for the things and the people who bring you joy. Reflect back to others the love you receive from them. Smile and let your heart overflow with happiness.

You are important. Unique.

For in this way you are a shining example of one of the greatest gifts ever given.

The gift of genuine and unselfish love.

**Actions Speak Louder than Words.**

**A personal reflection on 1 Corinthians 13.**

At our core humans are driven by the need for connection and love. Our true nature is to be caring and compassionate. Most people have these core values.

Love is an active quality. It makes itself known in the actions that go alongside the words. It is one thing for a person to say, "I love you", but our actions towards those we say we love will show if those words are genuine or not.

Actions speak louder than words, and that is true whether we do something large or in the smallest of personal ways to show genuine care and love.

You know the Bible says even if you have special gifts but don't have love, you are just being a big and noisy nuisance.

It is at 1 Corinthians 13:1: "If I speak in the tongues of men and of angels but do not have love, I have become a clanging gong or a clashing cymbal."

Clanging and clashing noises. Ouch! It is the sort of discordant noise that gives other people headaches.

The Bible tells us that humans were created in the image of God (Gen 5:1), and that "God is love" (1 John 4:8). Quite simply Love is, because God is. Love was the gift of God. Without it, the original perfect man and woman could not have been made in God's image and likeness.

It is why we can show love to others. I think 1 John 4:19 puts it very succinctly when it says, "We love, because he first loved us." At 1 Corinthians 13:13, the Bible tells us of the many gifts that one can possess, the greatest of these is Love.

Love is evident when it is seen. How then can we display Love in our day-to-day lives? I can think of no better way for me to close this personal reflection with the description written in the Holy Scriptures at 1 Corinthians 13:1-8.

"If I speak in the tongues of men and of angels but do not have love, I have become a clanging gong or a clashing cymbal. And if I have the gift of prophecy and understand all the sacred secrets and all knowledge, and if I have all the faith so as to move mountains, but do not have love, I am nothing. And if I give all my belongings to feed others, and if I hand over my body so that I may boast, but do not have love, I do not benefit at all.

Love is patient and kind. Love is not jealous. It does not brag, does not get puffed up, does not behave indecently, does not look for its own interests, does not become provoked. It does not keep account of the injury. It does not rejoice over unrighteousness, but rejoices with the truth. It bears all things, believes all things, hopes all things, endures all things.
Love never fails."

# BLESSINGS

**Blessings Every Day.**

My alarm sounded this morning.
I am blessed to have ears that hear

I opened my eyes.
I am blessed to have the gift of sight

I sat up in bed
I am blessed to have a comfortable place to sleep

I swung my legs to the floor
I am blessed to have legs that carry me

I looked around the room
I am blessed to have a room and indeed a roof over my head

I opened the curtains and looked out of the window
I am blessed to have hands that do the work
And blessed to have a house with windows to keep out the rain

I put on the bedside table lamp
I am blessed to have a home with electricity

I went into the bathroom to relieve myself and wash my hands
I am blessed to have hot running water, access to soap, and the luxury of a
flushable toilet
I am blessed to have the sense of touch, as I lather my hands

I came down to the kitchen, got the cereal box out of the cupboard and put the
coffee pot on
I am blessed to have the means for sustenance readily on hand

Ah the smell of freshly brewed coffee
I am blessed to have the gift of smell
And the gift of taste as I drink my coffee

Sitting at the table I eat my breakfast cereal
I am blessed to have a place for eating

I listen to the morning's news on the radio, and sing along with the jingles
I am blessed to have a means of learning about the world
And the gift of speech
And a mental ability to recall and recognise musical tunes

This list could go on and on.

It is easy to take it all for granted, the routine of waking, eating, dressing, our everyday activities. Yet each of those actions, yes at times carried out automatically by us without much thought on our part, is a blessing, a miracle, a special gift to be savoured.

Compared to so many inhabitants of the world we are blessed people with our homes and our possessions. It is likely most mornings we take it all for granted and fail to see it for what it truly is, a blessing.

With practice we can learn to express gratitude for the many gifts that we possess. Now, whether we believe in a God who has granted us such things, or whether you believe it is Mother Nature, or the Universe, it is good to give thanks. Even if we believe it is all down to our own hard work and good fortune, it is still beneficial to us to acknowledge that we are blessed.

There are many, many, people globally who, even as you are reading these words, are scraping a living in dire circumstances or struggling to survive in those lands presently enduring famine, natural disasters, or warfare.

Even if you are in poverty in this land, and there are many nowadays who with rising food prices and living costs are, you can still be grateful for what you have and the measure of health that you possess even if it is in poor condition.

This is your life….

Acknowledge it
Appreciate it
Cherish it
See the potential within it
Express gratitude for it
Reach out to those around you
Celebrate with them the gift of life
Celebrate the smallest of achievements
And if your mental health allows for it, try to be happy
Smile
Look at your life to see each blessing received daily.
Then each new dawn will grant you a fresh start to practice gratitude
For every day is a gift
The gift of life.

**Written After the Loss of My Grandmother.**

I have gathered my memories here of all the happy days we spent together
When you shared your stories and your edited history
As we pored over photographs of a much younger you
To the soundtrack of your loud ticking mantel clock.

You taught me forgotten skills as you poured endless cups of tea
And always just happened to have a slice of my favourite cake on hand as if by magic
It's only now I wonder what you had to go without to make it happen
On the weekends that I visited you at Number 187.

You wrapped me up when I got soaked playing in the rain
You tucked me up when my dreams were filled with pain
You carried me to bed when I was a little child
You gently chastised me if I got a little wild.

And now that you are no longer present
I cherish the precious times we shared together
I carefully return to each fragile memory of mine
Like those faded petals in the flower press you once gave me.

And I instantly see your smile and hear your laughter
I recall your delight in our smallest achievements
I can sense your protective arms still circled around me
You will never die as long as I am alive as I tell the world about you.

**My beautiful grandmother Sarah.**

"Recovery Is Never Easy".

The following poem was inspired by the journeys of people that I have met in support groups who have been able to turn their lives around. It is a compilation of many of the sad and heartbreaking accounts people were able to share. They might have been given assistance by healthcare professionals and other people but at the end of the day it was the individual's desire that got them to where they are today. Every one of them is a champion and a winner. I applaud them all.

---

**Recovery is Never Easy.**

Your mother was beaten
By your father, a drunk
His brother was a priest
Before doing a bunk
Those earliest memories can
Hurt you so much
You end up in therapy
Though it's merely a crutch
Only you know the full trauma
Nobody tells you how to say
What gives you the strength
You have to this day
Nobody digs deeper
Than you will yourself
To exorcise dark demons
That were left on a shelf
In childhood when you
Were systematically hurt
Where so-called protectors
Treated you daily like dirt
For decades you've carried
The stigma and shame
The bastards are dead now
They each played their game
The suffering you suffered
Ingrained in your pores
Still spills out unexpectedly
Like some toxic spores
But inside yourself you know
You truly are good
You try your damned hardest

To function as you should
And if you are winning
It's because you have fought
Not to become them through
The way you were taught
By fists and by hitting
By slaps and by slander
By kicks and by spitting
To push you down under
Yet you managed somehow
To grow a thick hide
To deflect savage blows
And stay bravely inside
It's a wonder you're living
It's great that you're sober
Your support of real friends
Has helped you start over
So, hold up your head
With strong heart stand straight
You're amazing my friend
As a survivor, you're great
Your example inspires others
For your story rings true
To come from that childhood
We're truly very proud of you.

**A Sinner Repents and Asks God for Mercy.**

Dear Heavenly Father oh please hear my plea
I have great need of forgiveness from thee
I have strayed far from your holy track
Please dear Father guide me back.
I searched for fame, but it was denied
I sought out pleasures and those I tried
I sunk so low into this world's mire
My situation was worse than dire
And yet in that my darkest hour
I sensed a presence, a strength, a power
And childhood prayers through lips I mumbled
A heartfelt realisation that I had stumbled
I turned my back on this filth and said
Let me seek you Lord or I'll be dead
Forgive me Father for I know I've strayed
Let me come back home is what I've prayed
Oh, save me Lord, my Lord above
For you I know are the embodiment of Love.

A little background to this next piece of poetry – "Our Prayer for You".

As a published poet I was contacted one day through email by a Christian friend of a friend who lives in the Philippines. A member of their family was getting married, and she wanted to read the newly-weds a poem about love and marriage. She had looked at various published examples, but they didn't meet with her approval. She asked me if I could assist by writing a poem in English for the occasion. I said that I would be delighted to help.

I obtained further information about the couple, their hopes and dreams, their names, and their faith in God. It took me quite a bit of time, and several attempts before I was content with it. I sent it off for her approval and after a few minor amendments she was happy.

It was my pleasure to write and that it was appreciated by the couple on the big day was reward enough for me. I have removed the personalised details from the poem, but the remaining verses are set out below.

If any of you would like to use it for a wedding service you are attending, you are welcome, please go ahead and do so with my blessing.

**Our Prayer for You.**

The wedding service ends with a loving kiss
Going forward please remember this
Almighty God provided marriage as a gift [1]
Something beautiful to uplift
Two individual people joining as one [2]
Today your new adventure has just begun.

Who can understand how love grows? [3]
Working together and blessings flow [4]
Two are better than one, the Bible reads [5]
Render to each other according to your needs [6]
And as you progress and find your feet
You'll realise that now you are complete.

Along with much joy there may come pain [7]
Amidst the sunshine there is also rain
But God holds you both in His warm embrace [8]
He's there beside you no matter what you'll face [9]
As you marry today surrounded by your many friends
We wish you both the deepest love that never ends. [10]

[1] Genesis 2:18.
[2] Mark 10:7,8.
[3] Proverbs 30:18,19.
[4] Proverbs 18:22.
[5] Ecclesiastes 4:9.
[6] 1 Corinthians 7:3.
[7] 1 Corinthians 7:28b.
[8] Deuteronomy 33:27a.
[9] Ecclesiastes 4:12.
[10] Song of Solomon 8:6,7 and Colossians 3:14.

**A Personal Message for You.**

You are not your struggle
You are not your fears
You are not your past mistakes
Please wipe away the frequent tears.
You are good, you are kind,
You were born to grow and flourish
You are strong, you are brave,
You are someone that we cherish.
You are not your partner's faults
You are not your parent's sad addiction
Do not let anyone gaslight you
For any words you hear are fiction.
You are not your traumas past
You are not your darkness nor your shame
You endured the pain you've been through
Now's the time for you to reign.
You have chosen this recovery journey
You are someone with a future bright and free
Where you'll experience love and contentment
As you shout out proudly "Yes, this is me!"

**Showing Love to Someone with Depression.**

Pick me up if I can only crawl
Catch me please if I should fall
A box of tissues if I start to bawl
And answer me if I might call.

You have no need to worry friend
This struggle is hard but it's not the end
I am happy a helping hand to lend
And anything else if I can, I'll mend.

I feel a failure I'm so sad
Nothing is good it's all quite bad
Perhaps I'm slowly going mad
When I do then you'll be glad.

Come now my friend stop this refrain
You only want to end your pain
It's obvious to me it is very plain
I'm here for you and will be again

I am here and not going away
I'll guide you through the roughest day
Right beside you is where I'll stay
You will get better I know and say.

When you are in a deep dark place
And turn your back on the human race
A treasured friend will see your face
Those special people you can't replace.

Every day they're there for you
Hug you tight and help you through
So, stick to them like super glue
Because such friends my friend are very few.

**If Only We Had Known.**

Let us pause a little while and bow our heads
To remember those who are no longer with us here
Who felt there was no other way through
Or in anguish simply wanted their pain to end.

Those who didn't get an intervention at the crucial moment
Who mislaid the helpline number and couldn't find it
Or didn't use it in their hour of need
Because their mobile phone was out of charge.

Those who didn't have real friends to call upon
Or whose friends told them to wise up and catch themselves on
Or who didn't want to bother anyone with their woes
Not even mum or dad or other siblings once again.

May we not forget about the many families and relatives
Who now live with their own dreadful pain of regret and loss
The emotional turmoil of both anger and sadness
Daily gnawing at their mind.

If there are words of prayer you believe are appropriate
Perhaps, quietly to yourself, you can say them now,
Or simply bow your head in a moment of silent reflection
For if only we had known.

"The Good Samaritan."

This poem is not about me. It could have been at one time in my past, but it isn't.
It is a mash-up of the journeys of a few people whose stories I was privileged to
hear in support groups. Plus, a little bit of poetic license thrown in as well to ensure
the anonymity of the people involved is kept.

I can tell you that it took me a couple of weeks of writing and redrafting before I
felt I had got it right. My desire is that you will never forget the message in this
poem as it may one day help you save another person's life or maybe even your
own.

**The Good Samaritan.**

It was a stranger who asked me my name
He said that he could see my pain
You appear to be in a dark place, again?
So let me get you some help my friend.

I always found it strange you know
That colleagues, friends, old so-and-so
Could tell me my targets were below
But were unable to see my woe.

We came and went or stopped for tea
Yet those who knew me just didn't see
That I was no longer the same happy me
How trapped I was, wanting to be free.

How I was sliding into a deep dark pit
And yet nobody else had the wit
To say to me "what's wrong with you?"
Or recognise that I was feeling blue.

It took a stranger, whom I'd never seen
He simply stopped and so serene
He wasn't blunt, he wasn't mean
He asked me gently how I'd been.

And like a floodgate broken free
It all came tumbling out of me
How in despair I could not see
Because depression was engulfing me.

Quickly he took me to a hospital then
And explained my situation to the men
Apart from saying his name was Glenn
I doubt I would even know him again.

The moral of this story is quite plain
If you see a person who looks in pain
Stop please just ask them to explain
How they are feeling and then remain.

It might make the difference between
An injury, life, or a death obscene
You have a chance to intervene
Don't dismiss it simply as routine.

Maybe you'll get "clear off pal" or a yelp
Not everyone will want your help
But perhaps if only just the one is willing
That's another soul who will keep living.

## Do You Hear the Wings of Angels?

The children run into the playground
Sliding down and swinging high
Climbing up and being childish
The way that only kids can be
Laughter reigns and lots of squealing
Giggles from the sandpit square
A child goes higher in her swinging
And launches outwards into air
Tumbling, falling, crying, screaming
All heads look up and mouths drop down
Injury or worse will follow
As she hurtles to the ground
Teachers standing on the edge immobile
Every person paralysed in shock
Perhaps one praying for them all
Yet suddenly the frantic child
Has been safely neatly caught
In the arms of a passing stranger
Who claims his presence a stroke of luck.
Everyone is fussing over her now
Soothingly speaking, calming down
The children all go back to playing
Games resume and happy laughter
But when someone turns around
To genuinely thank that stranger
For his quickness and strong arms
He is nowhere and can't be seen
Though the streets are wide both sides
Of the school in open view
Can you hear the wings of angels?
Quietly on the morning breeze.

**When the Mucky Stuff Hits the Fan.**

There's a secret to being happy
First of all try not to be sad
Think about the good times
Don't think about the bad.
Think about the people you love
The ones whose memories make you glad
The fun or adventures you enjoyed together
And you're so happy that you had.
Think about the many reasons
You are grateful in your life
Maybe you have a comfy home?
Or children? employment? savings? perhaps a wife?
Happiness isn't a one-off thing
It isn't a magic wand we can wave
It's a collection of the good times in life
That you need to bank and save.
When the bad days come, for they will of course
And it seems like a crash is near
Then you can live off the interest banked
To be happier without fear.
And even if you have the worries
When fear refuses to go away
This is still the route to happiness
Be grateful if even it's only for one day.

**Loving Life the Way I Like to Live It.**

I like the smell of rain falling on the garden soil, the soothing sound of waves reaching the beach. I adore the touch of the woman I love. Seeing her face brightens my day and with her smile l feel all warm and cosy inside.

My soul is lifted when I am in the company of dear friends. I delight to hear playful laughter from young children. I like the fresh subtle scents of garden plants, especially old roses, of herbs such as thyme, lavender, rosemary, though I like the heady stronger scent of white lilies as well.

I like gentle strolls. I love the woodlands or sitting quietly beside a flowing stream. I enjoy browsing around antique shops or second-hand bookstores, even if I buy nothing. I like to read, learning something new each day even if it is only one new word for my vocabulary. I like to spend time with my favourite books, reading them many times, similar to meeting up with old friends.

I allow myself to be embraced by music letting it transport me to memories of the past. I love to write poetry or verse, even if no-one else will ever read my words.

I enjoy the smell of coffee brewing first thing in the morning. The smell of bread baking in the oven. The scent of soap as I wash my hands after working outside. The texture of a pebble I find on the beach. The smell of soup, stew, or jam being made on the kitchen stove. The taste of the first peas plucked from the stem in our vegetable garden.

I like sitting at the window on rainy days just watching the puddles grow. On winter nights feeding the fire with logs, as the flames cast dancing shadows around the darkened room. In summer, relaxing outside soaking up the healing rays.

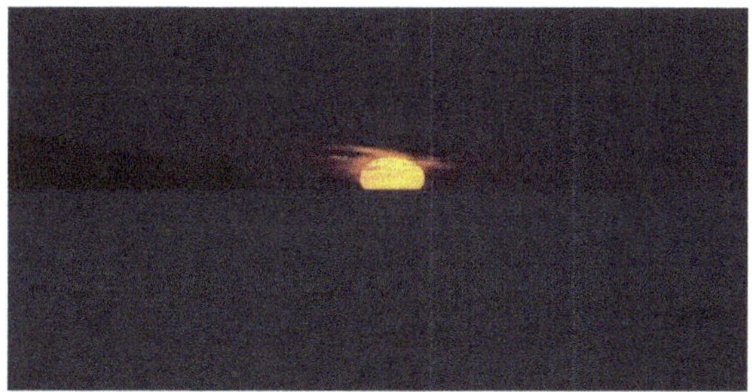

I love watching the big fluffy clouds floating by up above, or sitting quietly as the sunset lights up the sky before the sun slowly sinks down below the horizon line. At times like this I feel I am in the presence of the Divine.

I like all these activities, the simple things that remind me that life is beautiful. That I don't need to make it complicated to enjoy it to the fullest. I don't need to travel very far to find wondrous things, pleasant experiences, and enjoy the emotions that accompany each one of them.

**On Mother's Day.**

She is the one who gives you life
Brings into this world your form
Some of them will stay beside you
With cuddles to keep you warm
Others display neglect, are bad
Yes, even outright cruel
Contrasting with those who show deep love,
Are kind, taking you to school.

Why are some people's mother's different in these ways?
Nature, nurture, or genetics, I guess
Personality, history, addiction, abuse,
All must play their part, although I confess
I don't know how it happens
Other than the sad fact it does
And children grow up, molded
Through these experiences and loss.

Which is why to many folk
That cry of "Happy Mother's Day"
Will have them weeping salty tears
Because their childhood never was that way
Yet for others those same three words
Will never make them glum
But bring forth pleasant smiles and joy
Memories of the marvellous woman they call Mum,

Who brought them into the world
Who brought them joy to know
Who taught them wrong from right
And comforted them when low
We know of someone who,
Though mistreated and beaten,
Has in adulthood reached out
To connect, and say 'Mum, you are forgiven'.

For others that's a hill too steep
To climb and one they never will
Daily wishing her harm and death instead
And even fantasise about her kill,

What is sad and on this I dwell
As little children suffer from this abusive state
They have to carry it into adult life
Unresolved trauma, PTSD, and hate.

Sadly, we can't decide the family
Into which we will be born
We must make the most of things
And weather through the storm
Thankfully and from the heart
I can truthfully say
I was born into a loving family
With love and in God's way.

Who taught me to value truth
Display a love to others too
Develop personal values
To carry my whole life through,
I was very blessed I know
With parents who loved me dear
For them I am thankful not one special day
But on every day, I live each year.

My lovely mum and myself many moons ago. She enjoyed knitting as is evident in this photograph, and many other photographs in our family album.

**This is Only Temporary.**

Some days our life is full of fog
Our brain feels mush, our mind is clogged
We struggle on bravely yes despite
And hope beyond hope for some respite
One foot placed in front of the other
Before everything becomes too much bother.

But above us a light is glowing bright
To show the way through this darkest night
And then fog changes slowly into mist
Until our bad days can be dismissed
Our steps begin to be a little stronger
And we will live a few years longer.

"Therapy, For You or Not?"

Some people find going to mental health related therapy and unravelling the memories from their past to evaluate them in the present light works well for them. It sets them free and helps them to move on with their lives. Others who have taken part in such activity have found themselves overwhelmed by the process and ended up in a worse frame of mind mentally.

Of course, obviously it must be a personal choice. You must not allow anyone else to pressure you into doing such work if you genuinely believe that it isn't right for you (or perhaps just not at this stage in your life) or let them put you off doing it if you feel it is what you need and is going to be therapeutic or cathartic for you.

The following poem is about weighing up what is important to you. It is not to be taken as advising anyone else on the course of action to take when it comes to deciding on whether to engage in therapy. At the end of the day, what I have written is only a poem.

**Therapy, For You or Not?**

There's a secret trapdoor in your mind
That leads to steps which wind and wind
Ever downward through the dark recesses
Forbidden rooms and tunnel trespasses
Into forgotten places where lurk memories
Far away from the safety of your cameras
Therapy peeling back layers for your good?
As long as you first understood.

That the traits from a very early age
Moulded your characteristics to engage
Buried under sediment of deep regret and pain
You need to carefully watch your steps again

If necessary, stop and excavate a stony rockface
Or perhaps the demons hidden there embrace
And send you running out in abject fear
In case the darkness would reappear.

Therapy can be both charm or snake
But the choice is always yours to take
Sometimes it is better to walk in the light
Without knowing what caused the blight
Because an opened grave can disperse germs
Which once again can cause great harms
You carry all this from your childhood mind
Where environment was perhaps unkind.

Back when a tiny child had no choice
Perhaps you didn't even have a voice
For in order to survive and cope
You buried the bad and held a hope
That one day everything would be alright
You'd move from darkness into the light
And then as successful adulthood loomed
Your nightly dreams were full of gloom.

The little child you'd hidden away
At times prodded you hard to have a say
Until at last you crumbled under this stress
Thinking it was time now surely to address
This darkness lurking in your soul so deep
To make a final once clean sweep
When honestly it may be more sweet
To bury it deeper under tons of concrete.

To forget the past and enjoy the present
Let go of everything that you resent
Because what the mind dwells upon it energizes,
Including those dire dark feelings in all their guises
Whereas your energy could be better spent
On the restful things which make you content
And raise your vibrations, embrace the light
Live in the moment and sleep well at night.

It is vital to make your self-care a priority. Self-care is not being selfish. Taking a break shows that we love and value our self. Schedule personal time by marking it out on your calendar as you would any other important appointment. It isn't always possible to get outside in nature, so make a list of things you would enjoy just as much, such as a massage or a long soak in the bath or sitting in a comfortable chair with a good book and a cup of your favourite beverage. Even just retiring to your bedroom and hanging a "do not disturb" sign on the outside of the door to take an hour purely for yourself. The important thing is that you make it a regular practice. Your mind and body will certainly thank you for it.

## Mirror, Mirror on the Wall?

I often wish I could make a mirror
That showed the viewer how well they do
Despite the obstacles in daily life
Their courage always would show through.

We stand most mornings, a daily rite
To stare at our face there reflected
Berate ourselves for imagined imperfections
And list off things we have neglected.

Such as "I'm disappointed with myself."
"Nothing feels worthwhile anymore."
"What's wrong with me, am I stupid?"
"I wish I were on a different shore."

Is it any wonder that life's a grind?
With exasperation following on from regret
That daily ritual at the mirror
Is something you need to forget.

How better it would be with a reframed mirror
To remind you daily of how great you are
Highlighting your strengths and inner wisdom
Your attributes and your mental power.

Wouldn't that be so much better
And set you up for a positive day
Starting tomorrow in front of your mirror
Think about positive things to say.

Your mantras could be "I am worthy"
"I choose my destiny" or "People love me"
Repeat them daily, with strong conviction
And live each day with positivity.

**Love is….?**

If your roses were black
And your violets were green
Och well, never you mind.
After all, it's the thought that counts
And your Romeo, for all you know
Might simply be colour blind.


**A Word of Advice to All the Single Women.**

Dear ladies, I offer this advice with the utmost of tact
Because I know it is true and indeed is a fact
If searching for a lover, please choose the right one
The worst possible outcome is stuck with a right one!


Him: I love you. I would swim a crocodile infested river to you, scale the
highest mountain, cross the deepest ravine on a tightrope....

Her: Will I see you tonight?

Him: Yes. As long as it doesn't rain.

**Be in Love with Your Life Today.**

A personal reflection.

In the Holy Scriptures, Psalm 90:10 reads, "The span of our life is 70 years, or 80 if one is especially strong. But they are filled with trouble and sorrow; They quickly pass by, and away we fly."

It's strange. Did you know that in poverty-stricken countries of the world such as South Sudan the life expectancy today is still only around 62 for men and 68 for women? Yet that is DOUBLE or TRIPLE the life expectancy of the average citizen who lived back in the Middle Ages, where plague, hunger, and warfare, also meant there was an extremely high percentage of infant mortality. People tended to pack a lot into the years available to them in olden times!

We are conditioned to think about modern science, medical procedures, and medicine extending our span of time upon this earth. We probably know of several friends who are in their 80s, 90s, or even have made it to the century. Yet, as the Psalmist quoted above said, their years have been painful and not trouble free.

When you are a teenager life seems to stretch out ahead of you like an endless river. But there is no guarantee that one will grow old. Death can befall younger ones too without a warning. Likely we have heard of young fit sport stars dropping dead because of what is called "adult sudden death syndrome."

Sometimes, thinking that we have all the time in the world to do things, we put off the adventures we should be undertaking when we have the strength and energy of our youthful years. As time passes and realisation dawns, we can be filled with regrets and sadness. When we reach our 7th decade upon turning 60 suddenly life seems to have foreshortened very quickly. We start to make plans, hoping for enough energy to fulfil them.

Sometimes unexpected illnesses like stroke, heart attack, or cancers pull us up short as if to say: "And where did you think you were going so fast?" Certainly, it knocks the wind out of your sails so to speak, as I know only too well from my personal experience!

And what about when life ends? Ever since the dawn of civilization humans have laid their dead loved ones carefully to rest, be it in caves, cairns, graves, or crypts. There's an overwhelming sense of loss. Which is why most cultures carry a belief that life continues, whether that is by a future resurrection from the dead or by the journey of an eternal spirit to somewhere else. Tir-nan-og, Valhalla, the happy hunting grounds, the summer isles, paradise, to name but a few named locations in myth, history, culture, and deeply held religious belief.

Of course, whatever one believes the fact remains that death ends earthly life. Once again, the Bible, this time in Ecclesiastes 9:5-7, spells it out: "For the living know that they will die, but the dead know nothing at all, nor do they have any more reward, because all memory of them is forgotten. Also, their love and their hate and their jealousy have already perished, and they no longer have any share in what is done under the sun. Go, eat your food with rejoicing, and drink your wine with a cheerful heart."

That is something to think about, isn't it?

Going about our day with a cheerful heart is much better than having a negative mindset.

For example, if you want to try some new activities or food, what is holding you back? Go on and do it.

Don't delay telling people the things you want to say to them. If you love them, tell them that you love them.

If you would like to reconnect with old friends or distant family, go ahead, what's stopping you?

If you want a close friend or family member to own some possession of yours after you are gone, set it in motion now.

Tomorrow is not promised to any of us. Live your life in gratitude and love.

And if all you want is to just lie down and rest today, it is your life, go do it with a happy heart and without regret.

Wishing each of you a truly blessed day.

**Danny and Mary.**

Danny and Mary had been going out for a while
He'd seen her at work, and he liked her smile
He asked her out and she had agreed
That's the way these things can lead.
They'd been dating for months and Danny thought
Perhaps it was time that he ought
To try and make it a permanent thing
Should he be buying an engagement ring?
On Thursday in Mary's flat drinking wine
Their conversation was going fine.
The liquor emboldened Danny to say
"What would you like for your birthday?"

Looking around, up, down, and at Dan
Mary said, "I really need a talisman."
"A talisman would bring me lots of joy,
What do you think, my Danny boy?"
It wasn't the answer he expected her to utter
Oh it left poor Danny in a bit of a fluster
"I'll see what I can do Mary" he said with a wink
But quickly poured himself more wine to drink.
Later at home he couldn't sleep
"Fancy her wanting a talisman to keep
A lucky charm of sorts, you'd wonder why?
But I've agreed, so more foolish I."

He trawled the Web and online sites
But nothing he saw seemed quite right
He wandered round many a New Age store
Until his feet were aching and his legs were sore
He asked of jewellers, but they all said no
His options he knew were running low.
With Mary's birthday approaching fast
Danny was looking even more downcast.
He heard of an eccentric guy from a friend
Who kept antiques and odds and ends
He rang and asked if he could come by
And explained to the man the reason why.

"Something every woman needs to own."
Replied the eccentric down the phone

Danny hurried to the dusty antique shed
The man had talismans of silver, gold, and red.
In the end he bought one of hallmarked silver
With a fanciful design like a flowing river
The seller said the wearer would be protected
And it cost Danny much less than expected.
He bought gift wrapping, a box and ribbon
To have it ready for the giving
And after work on Mary's birthday
He hurried round to her doorway.

Waiting until the party guests had gone
And the two of them were on their own.
Danny presented his gift with a flourish
"Here is something you can cherish."
She opened the gift carefully, especially the box
Then looked at Danny her face in shock
"What on earth is this weird looking thing?
I thought maybe you were giving me a ring."
It was Danny's turned to look confused
Was his special gift being refused?
"But Mary my love," Danny began,
"It took me ages to get you a talisman."

"I thought you said owning one was your dream."
Mary laughed, "O Danny, Danny you are such a scream,
You weren't listening that's what I think
Maybe you had too much wine to drink?
I'll tell you exactly what I said that night
You'll hear it from me, and you'll hear it right."
Danny found for once he couldn't speak
"Please tell me Mary," was all he could squeak.
"You were talking about us making a home
And I said it'd be great together to own
But what I needed Danny to make it worthwhile
Was for my tallish man to walk me down the aisle.

**Did I Ask to be Born?**

I sometimes hear teenagers and occasionally even people who are older lament and say, "I didn't ask to be born." It's true. None of us get to choose where or when we will arrive into this world.

But the fact that we have arrived is a miracle. The combination of your father's sperm to your mother's egg - all of us began our existence inside our mother's body as a single cell smaller than the period at the end of this sentence.

That microscopic cell was extremely complex. A miniature chemical laboratory which grew rapidly, so that by the end of your second month in the womb, your major organs were already formed. Genetic history and patterns from both sides of your parental lines were already determining some of your characteristics.

You, my friend, are a miracle.

 Just think, had you a different father say, your inherited genes could have been totally the opposite to those you have developed. You are a unique creation. Nowhere in this world is there another you. Even if you were born as an identical twin, you will be unique and separate from your other twin.

So, yes, you didn't ask to be born, but that you were born is a marvel beyond comprehension, you are so very special because no one else in this world is you. How does that make you feel?

The problem is that since childhood we've been told that we're just a child. We've accepted the common narrative that we've heard. What we should be told from the time we are able to understand the spoken word is that we are special, unique, unmatched, capable of action that no-one else can achieve because there is nobody else who is us. If we'd been told that, nothing would have stopped us striving for personal greatness.

However, it's not too late. Go for it now. You, my friend, you are not just one in a million, you are one. The only one. You are you.

My miracle friend, achieve your full potential because no-one else on this planet will ever be you. You are a miracle. You are unique. Sure, you never asked to be born. But you were.

And you were given as a gift to this world in this time and in this place. Please, go ahead now and acknowledge your unique divine heritage and venture forth. Who knows what you will yet achieve…

**Did Anyone in Your Family Have this Illness?**

I have for a long time now encouraged younger people to talk to their parents and grandparents about family illnesses while those older ones are still around. Because there will come a point in the future when some doctor who is treating you will ask you the question: "Did anyone else in your family ever have this illness?" And sadly, it is often the case that by the time you need the answer to this question the people who knew the answer, grandparents, parents, older siblings, are no longer alive or perhaps unable to remember because of dementia.

In our immediate and wider family circle there has been, or some are  still currently battling: stroke, heart disease, brain tumour, leukaemia, bowel cancer, pancreatic cancer, Parkinson's disease, diabetes, neurological movement disorders, chronic kidney disease, depression, osteoporosis, spinal compression fractures, shingles, high cholesterol, heart valve issues, complex ptsd, systemic lupus erythematosus, leg ulcers, gallbladder problems, malaria, blindness, osteoarthritis, scoliosis, anxiety, deafness, heart attacks, ocd, and anxiety.

What a list! I don't think I have left anything out, but I might have done. Can you begin to see why it's important to find out the family's medical history before it is too late?

Now you might wonder, apart from the obvious mental health conditions I have listed above, why do I advocate so much for mental health matters, when clearly our family are, or were, dealing with serious physical health problems?

The answer is simple.

Every major physical health condition someone is diagnosed with causes alarm and stress.

When my mum was diagnosed with leukaemia it came as a shock. The same was true when we nursed Pauline's daddy through his advanced cancer. I can remember him crying openly when I was with him in the consultant's room when Joe was initially told the bad news.

I can remember the anxiety I felt inside when I received a diagnosis of chronic kidney disease last year, coming on top of everything else caused by my earlier strokes!

Those familiar with our family will remember the frustration of my uncle Sammy due to the continuous whole body shaking of his Parkinson's… or the traumatic effect the death of his grandson 'wee Ross' had on everyone at the time that the child was undergoing his heart operation. And I could go on and on with lots more similar family accounts.

Just as mental health problems can cause physical health problems, the reverse is true. A diagnosis of a physical illness will often be the trigger for a mental health breakdown occurring.

I remember during a medical lecture (and I think it stuck in my head because of my late uncle) the Michael J Fox organisation stating that up to half of all people with Parkinson's may suffer from depression and/or anxiety at some point over the course of their illness.

Similarly, as Cancer Research UK state on their website - "feeling overwhelmed and out of control is common when first diagnosed with cancer. After a diagnosis of cancer, you might have a range of feelings including fear, sadness, anxiety and depression. These are normal responses to a stressful life experience."

And of course, the person who is the carer of the cancer patient will equally be trying to cope with the stress of it all.

We know what that feels like as Pauline had breast cancer in 2013, with

chemotherapy and radiotherapy treatment, and we almost lost her when she developed sepsis after her operation. Thankfully she is cancer-free after being given the all-clear by her consultant 6 years ago.

Sometimes the patient reaches an acceptance of their disease or illness, but it's the carer or partner who is liable to explode and rage at the slightest additional thing. Why? Because just as each of us has a physical health, we also have an emotional and a mental health which cannot be ignored and being the sole carer of someone you love can be a very stressful time.

Finding out details of your family tree has become an interesting hobby for many people. Equally important is finding out your family history when it comes to their health conditions, some of which can be hereditary.

It isn't being morbid to do it. In fact, it could be described as self-love, because one day in the future you will be glad you didn't procrastinate but took the time to chat to your family and relatives, to protect your future self.

In summary,

Do not put off asking those important questions.
Record or write down the answers you receive and store them somewhere safe.
Look after your own emotional health.
Learn tools that will help you manage your own mental health before the storms of life set in.
Never be ashamed to ask for help to protect your sanity, especially if other people rely upon you as their carer.
And finally, remember your own self-care because like the adage says, "you cannot pour from an empty jug".

**Count Your Blessings Before You Sleep.**

Let me be happy as this day draws to a close
Reflect on the good parts and dwell most on those
Count up my blessings as Mum used to say
Express my gratitude at the end of this day.

What brought me joy in the day that's just past?
What things did I practice I hope will now last?
Did I help someone by word, smile, or action?
It doesn't take long to do this reflection.

Psychologists tell us it strengthens the brain
Gratitude practiced neural pathways retrain
And as we prepare for another night's sleeping
Our mind is focused on memories worth keeping.

I've made it a habit and as I lie in my bed
I tick off the day's happy peaks inside my head
And as eyelids close, in my mind they are there
I'm grateful, yes thankful, and that is my prayer.

# Postscript

Someone asked me: "why do you support mental illness causes?"

Well, I support many different causes and charities covering a range of family illnesses (see page 71) and other endeavours close to my heart. But, yes, I do give much of my time to adult mental health services. I, along with my wife Pauline, volunteer with the Wellness Recovery Network (WRN) within the South Eastern Health and Social Care Trust (SEHSCT). WRN operates support groups and creative sessions across all areas of the SEHSCT.

Let me explain why mental health in particular matters to me.

It is because every physical illness impacts the mind. So, although a person might be struggling with (say) cancer, they will have thoughts about it which will involve their mental health.

Each of us has a mental health, whether it is good or not so good, in the same way we have a physical health. Unfortunately, many people forget this fact and that is why there is still a lot of unnecessary negative bias surrounding mental health.

Take someone who loses a loved family member in death. They may or may not have an immediate physical reaction, but they will certainly have a mental one!

In addition to the above, there are those mental health conditions which are diagnosed and must be dealt with long-term. Add to these the stressors which come upon people each day.

A recent statistic said that on average 1 in 4 people will have a mental health problem at any given time. Therefore, if you were to walk into a room with 60 people present, in theory, at least 15 of them could well have a mental health condition.

When I was severely ill with my severe clinical depression after losing my mum to leukaemia, I was grateful for the help I received from people working in the field of mental health.

I'll be honest with you. I wouldn't wish what I went through during my lengthy period of depression on anyone else but having gained this lived experience I can empathise with other people. By volunteering some of my strengths today I can give something back to help those people who are in a similar boat.

And that is why I support mental health causes.

A photograph of me giving my poetry reading at the launch of the Wellness Recovery Network in the City of Lisburn back in 2022.

A photograph of me presenting the Mayor of Lisburn with a signed copy of my poetry book entitled "Poems to Lift your Mood" back in 2022. All proceeds from the sale of that book were donated to the Wellness Recovery Network.

A treasured photograph of myself with my mum Mollie taken only a few weeks before she received her diagnosis of acute myeloid leukaemia at the Ulster Hospital.

None of us know what is coming round the next bend in our life,
that is why we need to be grateful for each day we live,
and to live life with love in our hearts.